The Owl
in the Yard

Photographs and poem
by: **June Kasperski Wild**

Some birds live in the country,
Some birds live in the city,

Some birds are big and hungry,
While some birds are itty-bitty.

People build houses all
over,
Those houses can push out
the birds,

4

If bird families can't find cover,
Then pretty bird songs won't be heard!

So...I built a birdhouse with my dad,
It really wasn't that hard,

We hung it, and waited,
so glad,
To see which bird might
live in our yard!

Our owl box in the back yard!

A year went by with no nest,
We thought our birdhouse
would stay vacant,

Our patience was put to the test,
Then one day,
  we looked up,
    in amazement...

10

A fuzzy round head poked out,
Through the hole we had drilled for an entrance,

For us there could be no doubt,
That an *owl* had become our tenant!

We researched his kind in bird books,
We soon found out his name was: *Screech*,

Eastern Screech-Owl
(Megascops asio) 15

We spent our days taking
long looks,
At his cute little feathers
and beak.

Then one day we realized there were two,
When we looked at two photos together,

This owl is more black and grey in colour.

This owl is more brown and gray in colour.

We had made a home for
a pair,
These two were birds
of a feather.

They came and they went while we watched,
And then we began to find pellets,

22

Made of fur and bones
that got squashed,
In a gizzard which would
then expel it.

The pellets showed us what owls ate,
owls ate,
When they flew on their nightly sorties,

This gray blob is an owl pellet. Owls don't have teeth to chew their food, so they swallow their prey whole or in large pieces. The next day, they spit out the parts that they could not digest such as bones, teeth, and fur, all smushed together, as a pellet.

We found mice, birds, and
fish from a lake,
And occasional cedar tree
leaves.

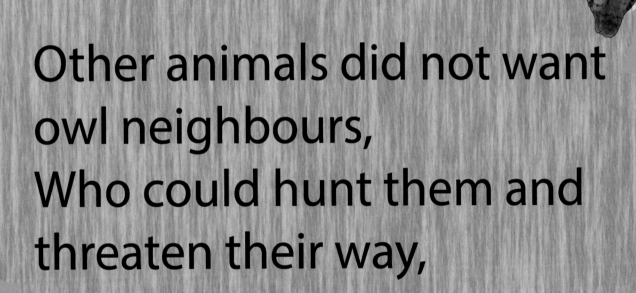

Other animals did not want
owl neighbours,
Who could hunt them and
threaten their way,

Bold chickadees do all the birds favours,
By trying to scare owls away!

The owl was just
sunning himself
one day...

When a Chickadee
came along and
chased him back
into his house!

30

We soon learned to take different paths,
On our daily search for their pellets,

Not wanting owls to incur wrath,
Of predators who saw where our prints led.

Some days when we went in the yard,
Walking around on the ground,

We'd look up the tree at the owl,
And the owl would be looking back down.

36

Finding whitewash led us to realize,
That the male spent his day hiding out,

Whitewash is like an owl's "poop" and will build up on branches and leaves underneath where an owl roosts (hides out) during the day.

Away from predators'
sharp eyes,
Waiting for the moon to
come out.

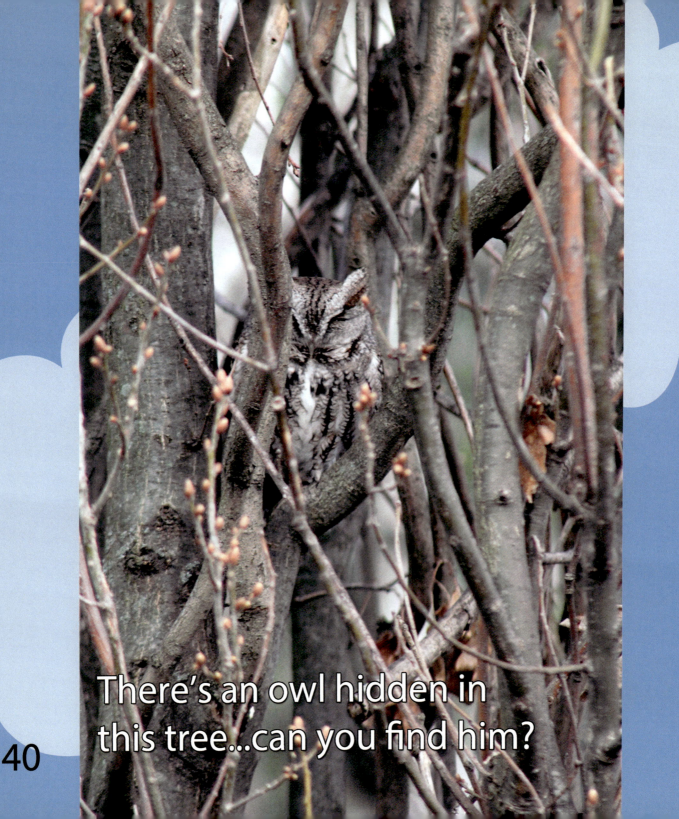

There's an owl hidden in this tree...can you find him?

We remember the day we looked twice,
At a small, downy head peeking out,

There must have been eggs hatched that night,
Owl babies had begun to sprout!

We had to discuss
what to do,
If one day a young owl
fell out,

Ending up alone on
the ground,
Without any parents
about.

We decided that a bird is best served,
By the care and attention of its family,

As people, we would
only observe,
Owl parents would handle
it handily.

Tired parents now spent
their days outside,
Away from the owlets' loud
squawking,

Sleeping while trying to hide,
Ignoring when we went by walking.

Sleepy parent on our window sill!

As the owlets grew big and grew strong,
Their parents began to encourage,

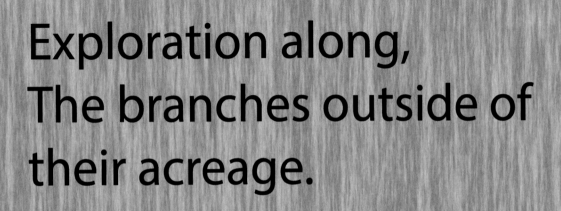

Exploration along,
The branches outside of
their acreage.

One-by-one they left home,
As each of them grew their
flight feathers,

As predicted, they were
seldom alone,
The family was often
together.

At twilight we'd sit on the porch,
As the parents flew off for the night,

To hunt in the dark, with no torch,
So their babies could each have a bite.

Then one night our porch-sit revealed,
That the family had moved out, for good,

Their nest box had lost its appeal,
They now lived in a nearby wood.

At first we were sad we weren't seeing,
The owls we had come to adore,

But their world was wild
and expanding,
So they didn't need our yard
anymore.

We know we were lucky to have owl creatures,
Living out back in our yard,

We had witnessed the
magic of nature,
And we hoped our owl family
would go far!

The Owl
in the
Yard

More Owly Fun!

Here's the poem, all in one place...

The Owl in the Yard

Some birds live in the country,
Some birds live in the city,
Some birds are big and hungry,
While some birds are itty-bitty.

People build houses all over,
Those houses can push out the birds,
If bird families can find cover,
Then pretty bird songs won't be heard!

So I built a birdhouse with my Dad,
It really wasn't that hard,
We hung it, and waited, so glad,
To see which bird might live in our yard.

A year went by with no nest,
We thought our birdhouse would stay
vacant,
Our patience was put to the test,
Then one day, we looked up in amazement...

A fuzzy round head poked out,
Through the hole we had drilled for an
entrance,
For us there could be no doubt,
That an *owl* had become our tenant!

We researched his kind in bird books,
We soon found out his name was: *Screech*,
We spent our days taking long looks,
At his cute little feathers and beak.

Then one day we realized there were two,
When we looked at two photos together,
We had made a home for a pair,
These two were birds of a feather.

They came and they went while we watched,
And then we began to find pellets,
Made of fur and bones that got squashed,
In a gizzard which would then expel it.

65

The Owl in the Yard
continued

The pellets showed us what owls ate,
When they flew on their nightly sorties,
We found mice, birds, and fish from a lake,
And occasional cedar tree leaves.

Other animals did not want owl neighbours,
Who could hunt them and threaten
their way,
Bold chickadees do all the birds favours,
By trying to scare owls away!

We soon learned to take different paths,
On our daily search for their pellets,
Not wanting owls to incur wrath,
Of predators who saw where our prints led.

Some days when we went in the yard,
Walking around on the ground,
We'd look up the tree at the owl,
And the owl would be looking back down.

Finding whitewash led us to realize,
That the male spent his days hiding out,
Away from predators' sharp eyes,
Waiting for the moon to come out.

We remember the day we looked twice,
At a small, downy head peeking out,
There must have been eggs hatched that
night,
Owl babies had begun to sprout!

We had to discuss what to do,
If one day a young owl fell out,
Ending up all alone on the ground,
Without any parents about!

We decided that a bird is best served,
By the care and attention of its family,
As people, we would only observe,
Owl parents would handle it, handily.

The Owl in the Yard

Tired parents now spent their days outside,
Away from the owlets' loud squawking,
Sleeping while trying to hide,
Ignoring when we went by walking.

As the owlets grew big and grew strong,
Their parents began to encourage,
Exploration along,
The branches outside of their acreage.

One-by-one they left home,
As each of them grew their flight
feathers,
As predicted, they were seldom alone,
The family was often together.

At twilight we'd sit on the porch,
As the parents flew off for the night,
To hunt in the dark with no torch,
So their babies could each have a bite.

Then one night our porch-sit revealed,
That the family had moved out, for good,
Their nestbox had lost its appeal,
They now lived in a nearby wood.

At first we were sad we weren't seeing,
The owls we had come to adore,
But their world was wild and expanding,
So they didn't need our yard anymore.

We know we were lucky to have owl
creatures,
Living out back in our yard,
We had witnessed the magic of nature,
We hoped our owl family would go far!

Remember those pellets?

We wanted to know what the owls were eating so we decided to dissect (take apart carefully) the pellets.

The pellets become a home for bacteria and parasites once they hit the ground. Some of these can hurt people, so we heated the pellets up in a covered dish on our barbecue to kill the things that might hurt us. Just in case, and to avoid breathing in anything harmful we used tools to touch the pellets and wore a mask.

Remember those pellets?

By using online animal skeleton glossaries, and matching what we found in the pellets to them, we were able to identify some of the animals eaten by the owls. Other things like feathers and claws gave us more clues. We learned that the owls were eating mice, birds, insects and even fish!

Bird bones

Bird claw

Insect shell

Feathers

Mouse tail

69

The grown-up owlets!

A few weeks after the owl family moved out of their nest box we heard a commotion in our back yard. The commotion was the sound of a group of smaller birds squawking and flying around trying to scare away the owl family. These are the last photos we took of the owl family!

Owlets with mostly adult feathers now!

Mother owl and owlet.

Would you like to make a nest box for your yard?

Having your own backyard bird adventure is as easy as 1-2-3.

1. We use the Cornell Lab of Ornithology's Nestwatch website to learn about nest boxes and participate in citizen science studies.
Go to: *www.nestwatch.org* and choose "All About Birdhouses" from the site contents. After we read the site and learned about keeping nests safe and how to build a nest box or bird house, we used the "Right Bird, Right House" interactive tool to figure out which birds were most likely to live in our yard and to find plans to build an appropriate nest box.

2. Out of respect for all of the wild creatures that you attract to your yard, it's important to remember that people can have an effect on how happy or stressed animals are. Photos should ideally be taken from a respectful distance, using a zoom lens, for short periods of time only. Grooming trees and/or the nesting area to get better photos and repeatedly taking the same path to and from a nesting area can alert predators to the location of the nest, often with devastating results!

3. If you don't have the resources or ability to build your own nest box there are lots of places where you can buy one. Try an internet search to find a retailer. If buying one is not possible, there are other ways to support the birds that visit your yard. Consider adding a water source that you keep clear all year round. This can be as simple as filling the drainage dish from a flower pot and balancing it on, or sticking it to its pot that you've placed upside-down on the ground as a base.

Have fun!

Photo Gallery

26766590R00042

Made in the USA
Middletown, DE
19 December 2018